Do It!

Six Steps to Happiness

Do It!

Six Steps to Happiness

by Winston K. Pendleton

CBP Press
St. Louis, Missouri

Unless otherwise indicated, all scripture quotations are from the Revised
Standard Version of the Bible, copyrighted 1946, 1952, © 1971, 1973, by the
Division of Christian Education of the National Council of the Churches of
Christ in the United States of America, and used by permission.

Quotations identified as KJV are taken from the King James Version of the
Bible.

Library of Congress Cataloging-in-Publication Data

Pendleton, Winston K.
　Do It!

1. Conduct of life.	2. Happiness.	I. Title.
BJ1581.2.P43　1986	158'.1	86-6112
ISBN 0-8272-0613-5		

Printed in the United States of America

To my dear friend
and a dedicated surgeon
EDWIN L. BRACKNEY
—
A man who
DOES IT!

Happiness is what you are,
not what you have;
What you give.
not what you get;
Not what somebody does for you,
but what you do for somebody else!

A Word About This Book

How do you feel?

Did you start today with a song in your heart? When you finally woke up and got started, did you feel *good all over?*

Were you thankful to be alive? Were you eager and ready to face the world with all of its joys *and its problems?*

Is your answer, "Yes"?

Congratulations! You've learned to *live.*

Welcome to another happy day.

Millions of people feel that way. They are in *control* of their lives. They do not allow outside influences—*other people*—to control their feelings—to destroy their happy day.

On the other hand, millions of people face each new day with little hope of joy or satisfaction. To them, happiness flits just out of reach, like a will-o'-the-wisp.

Why? What's the difference?

This book seeks to answer that question. It points to six steps that can lead anyone from a life of mental darkness and despair to days filled with spiritual brilliance and fulfillment. I call them the six steps to happiness.

The thoughts that you will find here did not originate with me. They came from the greatest book of inspired wisdom ever given to the human race—the Holy Bible.

May God bless you and strengthen you as you begin your journey toward happiness and a peace that "passes all understanding" (Philippians 4:7).

—Winston K. Pendleton

Add Your Own Thoughts

As you read this book, jot down your own thoughts at the end of each chapter. Your reading experience becomes richer as you add your own stimulating ideas. Keep the book near you. Refer to it often. Soon you will discover that the clouds in your life have disappeared and that the sunshine of happiness brightens every moment of your day.

Step Number One

Do you have trouble making up your mind? Is it hard for you to decide what you want to do—*and then do it*?

If that's one of your problems, you might find this first step the hardest to make. It calls for a decision. A tight, firm decision—*nailed down*.

There's an amazing fact about this decision. It carries a guarantee—an *unlimited lifetime warranty*.

But first: the decision you must make.

You must decide that you are going to live a fuller and more abundant life.

You must say, without the tiniest reservation, "I am going to find the way. And when I find it, I'm going to walk down it. And nothing is going to stop me."

That's easy to say. But it might not be easy to do.

Everybody, at some time, has trouble making decisions. Some people can do it easier than others. (They are the most successful people, as a rule.) But everybody faces that problem.

With the hundreds of decisions that people make each day, you might think they would learn to take them in stride, that they could decide something without a lot of fuss or bother, and without getting upset about it. And their decision making would become second nature to them.

But that's not so.

Even people who make decisions all day long sometimes get into trouble with decision making.

Nearly everyone has heard that old joke about the woman who was hired as a grader at a citrus packing and processing plant. Her job was to sit in front of two conveyer belts. Oranges flowed rapidly down the nearest belt, heading for the packing room, where they would be individually wrapped and packed in gift boxes.

She was supposed to grade the fruit as it passed in front of her. That is, she was to look for fruit that had any sort of scar or blemish on its skin. When she saw an orange that wasn't good enough to go into the gift box, she had to pluck it up and put it on the second conveyer belt, just a few inches away. Those oranges were diverted to the juice department, where they were made into frozen concentrate.

You wouldn't want an easier job. Right?

Not for her. After three days she quit.

When her supervisor asked why she was quitting, she said, "I'm almost a nervous wreck. All day long, hour after hour, I sit there making decisions. Decisions! Decisions! Decisions! I just can't work at a job with that much responsibility."

We laugh at the funny story, but maybe there's something that might be called "decision fatigue." Sometimes a person who makes decisions all day without any problem, suddenly can't seem to make a simple choice—often with upsetting results.

Here's an incident that happened to some friends of ours who live down the street. The story of the event and the dialogue are fairly accurate, although not word for word. Also the events of the day are given as a typical day of any suburban housewife, which our friend is. I'm going to call the couple Jan and Willard because that happens to be their real names. And so, to the happening.

You would never call Jan wishy-washy. Decisions? She made them all day long—quickly, efficiently, and with confidence. This particular day started out as usual. She was the first member of the household to get stirring. In and out of her shower in a hurry, she made her first decision: what to wear. Knowing this was her day to do her weekly shopping, she decided to wear a pink turtleneck sweater with blue slacks.

Her next decision was about breakfast. Cereal with a sliced banana for the two children. The same for her husband, plus a glass of prune juice. And when she heard the children moving about, she told them what to wear for school.

She even said to her husband, "If you wear your pinstripe suit today, be sure to wear a solid color tie—not that polka dot thing!"

That was just the beginning. Later, she decided which supermarket to visit, which brands and which sizes to buy. She made choice after choice in the produce department.

On the way home, she stopped at the library. More decisions. Six, in fact, for she checked out six books.

And so it went. No stress. No strain. She was a well-adjusted woman. She was an expert at making decisions.

But all that changed when her husband came home from work. As he did every day about 5:30, he parked his car in the garage and came through the back door into the kitchen.

"Hi, honey," he called.

"Hi," Jan said as she met him with a warm hug and kiss. "How did your day go?"

"Great! Super!" he said with a grin that almost split his face. "We had the final meeting on the shopping mall deal. And I'm ready to celebrate. I thought maybe I'd take everybody out to dinner tonight. How would you like that?"

"That sounds good," she said.

"Okay," he said, "Get Sue and Derik ready while I change into something more relaxing. Then let's go. I'm hungry."

Fifteen minutes later, the family was in the car, ready to go. Jan had changed her sweater and slacks for a dress, and the youngsters had combed their hair.

As Willard backed the car out of the driveway, he said, "Well, Jan, where do we eat?"

"Anywhere," she said, "It doesn't matter."

There it was!

Jan had been asked for a decision, and she backed away from it. She shied from it, not realizing the trouble she was leading into.

There are some who might say she made a decision not to make a decision, but that's begging the point. She was asked to *name a specific place*, and she refused.

"I thought we'd go up on Lookout Point," Willard said, "There are half a dozen good places up there. Or, we can run down to the beach. It's only twenty miles. What do you think?"

"Either one's okay," Jan said, "It doesn't matter."

What? No decision?

But Sue and Derik in the backseat made one. "Let's go to the beach," they said with one voice.

For the next twenty minutes, lively conversation made time pass quickly. Jan talked about their neighbors' plans for their daughter's wedding. And voices from the rear expounded on the day's activities at school and on the field day two weeks away.

Before they knew it—here was decision time again.

As their car rose high on the bridge across the inlet, the ocean was spread before them—clear to the end of the world. And each way, to the left and right, stretched miles of hustle and bustle: motels, hotels, condominiums, souvenir shops, beachwear shops, bars, and, of course, a few restaurants.

"Which way, Jan?" Willard asked. "North Beach? That's where the kids go. That's the noisy end. Some of the places have combos. Or would you rather go to the South Side and listen to piped-in music and eat with the senior citizens?"

"Either one," Jan said, "Whatever you want."

No decision!

But decision making seemed to come easy from the backseat. "We vote for North Beach," came word from Sue.

"Yeah, that would be neat," Derik said.

So they turned left and headed north up the main street, which was a block away from the ocean. Although it was not quite dark, the street lights and the neon signs on the business places had come on. Along the street and on ahead, the lights of a half dozen eating places were trying to entice customers.

Now, a time for more decisions.

"Where do we eat?" Willard asked.

Again Jan said, "It doesn't matter. Wherever."

And so it went. Willard and the youngsters picked out the restaurant. Ordering from the menu followed the same pattern. Sue and Derik ordered shrimp. Willard ordered pompano *en papillote* and Jan said, "That's all right for me too."

The meal went well. Conversation was animated and lively, and the service was excellent. Everyone seemed to enjoy the food, and few if any scraps were left.

What appeared to be a perfect day was drawing near a close. But wait! The day wasn't over yet.

The storm broke just after the family car had been parked in the garage and everyone was coming in the kitchen door.

"Home at last. It was a nice celebration," said Papa, rubbing his hands together and grinning like a little boy who had just won his fourth-grade spelling bee.

"Neat," said Sue.

"The shrimp was super," said Derik.

"It was all right," Jan said, "but we should have gone to Lookout Point."

"WHAT DID YOU SAY?" That was Willard.

(You'll notice he said it in capital letters. That was a signal for Sue and Derik to head for their rooms, to get out of the line of fire they sensed was coming. They were right. Here it came.)

"I said we should have gone to Lookout Point for dinner. You and the kids just had to go to the beach! I don't go much for seafood to begin with, and then that awful fish in a paper bag. Besides, the place smelled like dead fish. You might call it the tang of the sea, but to me it's just dead fish. Besides, on Lookout Point we can look down on the city and see the lights. It's beautiful up there."

"Hey, don't blame us. We asked you . . . ."

There's no need to go on with that conversation. You know how it went. "You said. I said. They said," and on and on.

You know how it started too. All because Jan wouldn't or couldn't make a decision. And that was a little decision.

What about big decisions?

Most big decisions develop and grow from little decisions. One decision leads to two more, and on and on. Like the man who decided to build a $300,000 house in Naples, Florida.

The decision might have been born twenty years earlier from an absolutely trivial choice—the decision between a hamburger and a fish burger. Picture this. Two men were headed back to their dormitory following a college basketball game in Ann Arbor, Michigan.

"Let's stop for a hamburger," said the first.

"Great!" said his roommate.

As they approached the quick-food restaurant, they saw the parking lot was overflowing and cars were backed up for half a block.

"Let's not get mixed up with that big mob scene," the first fellow said, "Let's go somewhere else."

"Right on," said his friend, "I've got an idea. It's five miles from here, but that new fish place just opened. They advertise fish burgers. Let's try that. Okay?"

"Okay," the first said.

When they arrived, there was no parking problem. And when they went inside, one of their friends, who was sitting at a table with a pretty girl, waved and invited the boys to sit at their table.

"Meet my sister," he said as he introduced them. "She came up to see her team try to beat our team. She's a traitor to the family, going to school in Ohio. But that's the way life goes."

And that *was* the way life went. Three years later, the young fellow who suggested the fish burger married the young lady. (A big decision from a little decision.) And seventeen years later, after tens of thousands of day-to-day decisions, he had become rich and had moved with his wife and children to Florida.

Now he had decided to build that $300,000 home, and with that decision came an additional 10,000 decisions—more or less.

What does all this have to do with you?

Nothing, really. Except that it shows that decision making is important; that nothing happens until someone makes a decision; and that every decision you make changes what comes next in your life.

That's the whole point.

You are faced with a choice. A choice that can change your life. A choice that can bring you much happiness.

You make choices all day long. Some are easy—like

whether you want toast made with white or whole wheat bread.

Big choices are not easy to make. They take much thought and discussion and prayer.

In his play *The Bending of the Bough*, George Moore put it simply: "The difficulty in life is the choice."

Books and poems and plays have been written about it. Shakespeare portrays Hamlet going through the agony of making a decision, saying to himself, "To be or not to be—that is the question. . . ."

Which step to take?

Robert Frost describes such a choice in the often-quoted poem *The Road Not Taken:*

Two roads converged in a wood and I—
Took the road less traveled by,
And that has made all the difference.[1]

That's your choice too. Which road to take?

You must make the decision. It marks your first step. You can't bypass it. You cannot begin any journey by skipping over the first step.

You must begin by making up your mind that *you will find happiness.*

Remember, earlier, when you were promised a guarantee? Here it is.

The guarantee for success comes from the Bible. Jesus said, "All things are possible to him who believes" (Mark 9:23).

If you believe strongly enough, Jesus says, you can do anything you think you can. You can become the kind of person you want to be. You can find happiness if you believe you can. If you have faith, you can move mountains.

That word *faith* frightens a lot of people. They think faith is some mysterious and unreachable attribute that lies just beyond the fingertips of man.

That's not true. You see faith everywhere.

If it is so common, what is it?

The writer of The Letter to the Hebrews gave the world the classic definition of faith. He said, "Now faith is the assurance of things hoped for, the conviction of things not seen" (11:1).

You see examples of faith every day.

According to the above definition, the woman who picks up a can of coffee in the supermarket illustrates perfect faith.

Does she fit the first part of the scripture definition of faith, "the assurance of things hoped for"? Certainly! She *hopes* the can contains regular-grind coffee and that it holds a full pound. She is *assured* that those things are true because the printing on the can says so.

How about "the conviction of things not seen"? Yes! She can't see inside the can, but she is *convinced* that it contains coffee. She does not question the manager of the store about its contents. She does not say to him, "Are you sure I'll find coffee and not sawdust in the can when I get home?" No! She displays 100 percent faith when she puts the can of coffee in her shopping cart.

Think how much better off our country would be if all of us had as much faith in God as we have in the company that grinds our coffee!

Faith exerts great force. Faith helps weak people become strong. Faith takes misguided and lost people and puts them on the right track. Faith shows defeated people how to win.

Faith lifts people out of the depths of despair and restores their hope. Faith leads unhappy and miserable people into a bright and glorious way of living.

Jesus said that faith can move mountains. That is true.

But a great many people misunderstand what he meant. Consider the woman who lived in Colorado within sight of Pike's Peak. She attended a church revival meeting once and heard the visiting minister preach on the power of faith. He quoted Jesus' statement that faith can move mountains. That night before she went to sleep, the woman decided to test that scripture. She prayed a seemingly fervent prayer, asking God to move Pike's Peak during the night.

When she woke the next morning, she rushed to the bedroom window and looked out. Of course, Pike's Peak rose up before her, as big as ever. And with a smirk, she said to herself, "I knew he wouldn't do it."

When Jesus said that faith could move mountains, he was speaking figuratively. He was saying that, even if your problems seem as high as a mountain, faith will help you overcome them.

On the other hand, if you want to take him literally, like the woman in Colorado, be assured that faith can move mountains—literally.

Look around. You see them being moved every day.

However, it takes a lot of faith to move a mountain.

First, if you want to move a mountain, you must *believe* that it can be moved. You can't think *maybe* or *perhaps*. You've got to *know* deep down in your heart that the mountain *can be moved.*

Next, if you can't move it by yourself, you must find help. The person who is going to help you, probably an earth moving contractor, also must believe that it can be moved. Not only that, he must have faith in his own ability to move it. More than that, you too must have faith in his ability, in his integrity as a businessman, and in his reliability.

But wait! That's not all.

The contractor must hire workers. He must have faith in the man who will operate the huge dragline and in those who will handle the bulldozers. These men, in turn, must have faith in the strength, efficiency, and durability of their equipment, which really means faith in the workmanship of the hundreds of workers who made the parts and assembled them.

Of course, in today's complicated world, you won't get far with your mountain-moving project without the 100 percent faith of your financial backers and your banker.

Yes, faith can move mountains.

However, when you are getting ready to move a mountain, remember exactly what Jesus said. He said, "all things are possible to him . . ." (Mark 9:23). He did not say, "all things will be given to him. . . ."

Now, as you think about finding a happier life, come back to the beginning—and that first question. Are you willing to take the necessary steps?

The first step is clear. Make up your mind to fill every day with happiness. Back up your determination with a strong faith. And keep in mind this guarantee, **"All things are possible to him who believes"** (Mark 9:23).

In his epistle, James made a plea for vital Christianity: "Faith without works is dead."

So, if you decide that you are going to take the first step,

Do It!

Notes of My Own

[1] From "The Road Not Taken" in *The Poetry of Robert Frost* edited by Edward Connery Lathem. Copyright 1916, © 1969 by Holt, Rinehart and Winston. Copyright 1944 by Robert Frost. Reprinted by permission of Holt, Rinehart and Winston, Publishers.

Step Number Two

Where are you going?

Step Number Two says you should know.

Ask your friend next door that question the next time you see her backing out of the driveway. She'll tell you.

She may be going to visit her hairdresser, going to the post office, or going to have lunch with a friend. She might even recite a dozen places she is going and things she plans to do.

One thing for sure: When she drives away in her car, she knows where she is going.

You'll never hear her say, "I don't know. I'm just going to drive around, I guess."

The next time you visit the airport, ask the same question of an airline pilot who is getting ready to take off. You'll be able to spot one. He'll be in uniform with a lot of gold braid on his sleeve, headed for the exit gate with a large black briefcase in his hand. Ask him.

He'll tell you. He'll be exact too. "We're taking off in twenty-three minutes for Los Angeles with stops in New Orleans and San Antonio. Flying time will be about five hours."

Can you imagine him saying, "I don't know"?

Imagine someone saying to the airline ticket agent, "I want a ticket, please."

When asked, "Where to?" can you imagine that person saying, "Nowhere in particular. Just a ticket. Anywhere"?

You would say, "Ridiculous! Stupid! Absurd!"

You would be right.

Such an attitude would be unthinkable. No airline could stay in business a single day without a definite destination for each flight.

People don't travel to "anywhere."

Take the matter of the average family going on vacation. The whole family gets in on the planning. They may spend weeks deciding where to go. To the mountains? To the beach? Abroad?

Once they decide where they want to go, they begin to talk about the hotels they will stay in and the attractions they will visit. By the time they are ready to leave home, they know exactly where they are going.

Yes, when it comes to travel, people make it a point to know exactly where they are going. And what's more, they know when they are going to get there.

That's so basically true that it seems silly even to talk about it. We wouldn't dream of leaving home without knowing where we were going.

When it comes to running errands around town or taking a vacation, we're superefficient.

Oh yes! We're well organized in America.

We're so well organized that we even plan for emergencies or digressions along the way. A homemaker might keep a casserole in her freezer, "just in case" company drops in unannounced. Or a businessman might carry a hundred-dollar bill in the "secret" compartment in his wallet "just in case." And that's why people carry umbrellas.

Let's take that airline pilot that we spoke about. He knew where he was supposed to go—his main goal. He knew when he was supposed to leave, how high and how fast he was supposed to fly, and when he was supposed to arrive. However, if something came up that interfered with any part of that plan, he was prepared to change it.

If he received word in flight that the airport at his destination, say Cincinnati, had been closed, he was prepared to land at Dayton or maybe Lexington. Certainly he would not say, "Since I can't land in Cincinnati, my flight is a complete failure. So, I will just fly until I run out of fuel and let the ship crash."

Or take the family that was headed for a week's vacation. They had planned a dozen places they were going to visit and all sorts of things they were going to do. So they weren't going to cry "failure" just because a certain amusement park was closed, a particular restaurant had gone out of business, or rain kept them from an outdoor picnic.

So, the airline flew their passengers to Louisville and bussed them to Cincinnati. They finally got them there, but maybe not in time for dinner. And the family had a great vacation trip, even though they missed seeing the elephant show.

Recently I attended a retirement banquet for one of the leading citizens of our town. For forty years he had taught agriculture in various high schools in the area. More than a hundred of his former students were in the huge audience. Eight or ten prominent people spoke that night, paying tribute to him and extolling his many virtues.

He was given a handsome plaque to hang on the wall of his den and he and his wife received a two-week Caribbean cruise.

I chatted with him about his successful career and asked him how he had decided to become an agriculture teacher.

"I didn't decide," he said, "I got into it by chance. You might say that circumstances decided it for me. I had dreamed of being a veterinarian. All through high school I planned to attend the College of Veterinary Medicine at the University. But when I arrived there to register, I was told that all the classes were filled.

"A friend of mine, standing next to me, was registering for the Agricultural College. He said I ought to sign up for that, and then I could transfer when there was an opening. So I did.

"Well, there wasn't an opening that year or the next. And I was more or less stuck in the Agricultural College. Later, I earned a master's degree in agronomy.

"Back in those days, jobs were hard to find. So I took what I thought was a temporary job as an agriculture teacher. And I've been doing that ever since. I've had a good life. I have enjoyed working with the youngsters. One of my students became state president of the Future Farmers of America. And any number of them have become highly successful farmers.

"I guess that's because I tried to teach them something more than agriculture. I have tried to implant in them the importance of having a goal in life—of deciding where they want to go, and sticking to it.

"I guess I have preached that to them pretty hard. Maybe because I've wondered what sort of veterinarian I would have made."

He would have made an excellent veterinarian, just as he had become an excellent teacher.

He was a success as a teacher, and he would have been a success as a veterinarian, because basically he was a successful man. He had discovered the *secret of success*—that is, if it is a secret: *Set a goal, and never lose sight of it.*

"Wait a minute," you might say, "He wanted to be a veterinarian. He ended up as a schoolteacher. That looks like he missed the boat. Why do you call him a success?"

He succeeded because his main goal in life was to become an excellent professional man. Along the way, he knew, he had to get a good education. And he did. He dreamed of being a veterinarian. But he made emergency plans in case he had to take a different path. And he did.

He would have been a failure if, when he found he could not get into the College of Veterinary Medicine, he had given up, returned to his hometown, and become a bum.

This raises the question, "What is success?"

Success has been defined many ways. The definition I like best is: *Success is the step-by-step progress toward your main goal.*

This is the way success is measured. A farmer might have a two-hundred-acre field that needs plowing. With his particular equipment, he can plow thirty acres a day with no trouble. So he plans to take it easy and plow twenty acres a day for ten days. His main goal is to plow the two hundred acres. His step-by-step goal is twenty acres a day.

He doesn't have to finish the entire two hundred acres in order to be successful. If he succeeds in plowing twenty acres that first day, he will have had a successful day. If he has ten successful days in a row, he will reach his main goal—two hundred acres.

But his goals must be flexible. Suppose it rains one day and he can't plow because the soil is too damp. Then, in order to reach his main goal on time, he'll have to revise his daily step-by-step goals.

We've talked about a farmer plowing his field, but the principle holds good for every phase of activity. A young woman may choose a career as a doctor or a nurse. A young man may want to become a teacher or an engineer.

In order to succeed, they must first set their main goal. Then they must determine everything that's necessary to reach that goal—how many years in school, which school, which subjects to take, which books to read, and so on. They then have to fix a timetable for success—what they are going to do day-by-day, step-by-step.

Once they have done that, and if they accomplish each day's goal, they will succeed. They will reach their big goal. *Nothing can stop them.*

The rule for success is simple.

Know where you want to go—*your main goal.*

Plan the steps you must take—*your intermediate goals*.
Set up a *success* schedule—*your day-to-day goals*.

Do it that way. If you accomplish today's goal, you will have had a successful day. Seven successful days will give you a successful week. Fifty-two successful weeks will give you a successful year. A lifetime of successful years will give you a successful life.

All of this is easy to understand when we are talking about plowing a field or flying an airplane or embarking on a college career. But what does all this have to do with learning to live a happier and fuller and more abundant life? The basic principle is the same. Yet millions of Americans are rushing through life, headed for *nowhere*. They live from day to day with no predetermined destination, with no definite *goal*. You must have a sense of purpose in your life—a definite goal, a spiritual and emotional goal.

This brings us to the main point in Step Number Two. What kind of life are you looking for?

The question now changes from "Where are you going?" to "Where do you want to go?"

That question concerns your spiritual life, not your career. Just because someone has reached the top of his profession doesn't necessarily mean he has found happiness, contentment, and personal satisfaction. Every day we read about people in high places—famous people, rich people, talented people—who live miserable lives.

Look at the rate of divorce among otherwise *successful* people. Couples who have learned to live together happily don't file for divorce.

Drug addiction doesn't respect any social or economic barriers, either. People who appear to have *everything* often turn to drugs in search of *something missing* in their lives.

Too often, people have worked so hard to achieve their material goals that they have overlooked the need to set spiritual goals.

Spiritual goals!

That's step two—setting those goals.

But how do you set a goal for something as intangible as inner peace or happiness?

The Bible holds the answer.

In Proverbs 23 we read that a person *is* what he or she *thinks* in the heart.

Think about that!

What an amazing statement!

That says you grow and develop into the sum total of your thinking. It says you will find happiness and spiritual fulfillment when you learn to think properly.

The key lies in your thinking.

The truth has been around for centuries.

Eighteen hundred years ago, Roman Emperor Marcus Aurelius wrote, "Very little is needed to make a happy life. It is all within yourself, in your way of thinking."

That sounds easy, doesn't it?

Think happy thoughts, and you'll have a happy day. Think unhappy thoughts, and you'll be miserable.

But it's not easy!

Emerson, one of America's greatest thinkers, said, "What is the hardest task in the world? To think."

He probably came close to the truth.

Because thinking is hard, it also seems to be relatively rare. The trend in America seems to be toward both *labor-saving* devices and *thought-saving* machines.

Take some of the new automobiles, for example. When you park some of the new models, a voice reminds you, "Remember not to leave your keys in the car," or "Your lights are still on." And some cars let you lock your car and walk away and not think about your lights. They are turned off automatically. No need to give it a thought!

That's great. It's a testimony to American inventive genius. But it's one more way that you are being discouraged from thinking. The only thinking in that case was done by the person who figured out how to turn the lights off automatically.

Sometimes, in spite of their best efforts, manufacturers have difficulty making things clear to their customers. Take the story about the man who ordered a self-powered, self-starting, leaf-pulverizing lawn mower. It was delivered unassembled. To make matters worse, the buyer was not the least mechanically inclined. The directions for assembling the lawn mower had been written by a *nonthinker*, who had not approached the problem from the point of view of the customer. The result became chaos on the floor of the customer's carport.

Finally, in desperation, he loaded all of the bits and pieces in the back of his station wagon and took them to his uncle's farm, some twenty miles away. There he asked his uncle's hired man if he could put the mower together and get it to work. The man said he'd try, and the buyer left the mower and drove back to town. When he arrived at home, he discovered that he had forgotten to leave the direction book with the hired man.

So he drove twenty miles back to the farm.

When he arrived there, he found the hired man happily mowing the front lawn with the new mower! Flabbergasted, he said to the hired hand, "How could you put it together so fast when I had the direction book?"

"Oh," the hired hand said, "It wasn't too hard. No need to leave the book. I can't read anyway."

With a puzzled look on his face, the mower owner said, "If you can't read, how did you manage to assemble the mower?"

"Well," the other replied, "I guess it's like this: If you don't know how to read, you have to know how to think."

Emerson was a great believer in the importance of thinking. On one occasion he said, "Great men are they who see that spiritual is stronger than any material force, that thoughts rule the world."

My first-grade teacher believed that. I don't know what they teach children today, but she tried to teach us to think. She illustrated the power of thinking by telling us the story about the little steam engine.

That was a long time ago, and I have forgotten the details, but I do remember that a big steam engine said that it couldn't take a certain load across a mountain. So it stayed in the station.

Then came the little steam engine. Obviously, if the load was too heavy for the big steam engine, the little engine wouldn't be able to handle it. However, the little steam engine said, "I think I can." And she hooked herself to the load and started over the mountain.

I can see my teacher now. I can remember that when she got to the part of the story where the little engine said, "I think I can," she began to imitate it. She shuffled and scraped her feet and went chug-chug-chug across the room. As she moved slowly in front of the class, she moved her forearms back and forth like the pistons of a steam engine and chanted, "I think I can, I think I can, I think I can, I think I can." Her rhythm matched exactly the sound of the trains that ran through our town.

That teacher knew how to inspire her students. She was able to stimulate our imaginations because she understood the power of thinking. When she gave a low "Whoo-eee, Whoo-eee," train whistle and called out to us, "Let's help her get over the mountain," you can picture what happened. We all jumped to our feet and began to work our arms like pistons. And some twenty or so shrill little six-year-old voices joined in the effort: "I think I can, I think I can, I think I can, I think I can."

For a few moments we became, in our minds, what we were thinking about—that little steam engine.

We honestly *believed* we were helping.

Guess what!

That little steam engine went right over the mountain without even stopping for breath.

Young minds seem more susceptible to suggestion than older minds. I remember the days before we had electricity in our home. My older sister and younger brother and I would sit on the floor close to my mother's chair after supper each night. By the light of the one kerosene lamp that was bright enough, she read to us. That was the nightly ritual, somewhat like Longfellow's "Children's Hour."

My favorite story in those days was Robert Louis Stevenson's *Treasure Island*. I think working her way through that story took my mother about a week.

There was no radio or television then, and only rarely were we able to scrape together the fifteen cents that would let us see a Charlie Chaplin or William S. Hart movie. So we each had to paint our own mental picture as the stories unfolded. We had to do our own *imagining*. We had to do our own *thinking*.

With no more responsibilities than the average eight-year-old living in a rural area, I had plenty of time during the day to relive the previous episodes of the story. Even in broad daylight, I would break out in goose pimples when I thought of Jim overhearing the pirates' treacherous plot while he was hiding in a barrel.

I dreamed of what might be coming next in the story as I stalked the pirates through the thick, flat hammock land behind my home. There were no hills or headlands from which to search out my enemies, so I climbed a huge old magnolia tree and set up my observation point in its tallest branches.

And for a time I was Jim, searching for buried treasure and beset by a gang of bloodthirsty pirates.

Really?

Certainly, as far as I was concerned because, as the scripture suggests, *you become what you think about*.

The power of thought works so strongly that it sometimes leads to tragedy and ruin. Fear is nothing but a kind of thought, often justified, but nevertheless, a result of thinking. The fear may come in response to a real peril or maybe some imaginary danger, but regardless of its origin, the fear itself is real because it's in the mind. Worry and anxiety are the fruits of thinking, usually thinking about terrible things that might happen—but don't.

Enthusiasm, too, and excitement are generated in the mind.

Thinking works in strange ways. Take what happens at a football game. Two groups witness exactly the same event. The final score can create a wild and joyful frenzy among the winning fans, *because of their thinking*. Yet the same score throws a damp blanket of gloom and despair over the supporters of the losing team, *because of their thinking*.

Thinking is the most important thing we human beings do. Nothing on earth was ever accomplished without someone's first thinking about it. Every masterpiece that was ever painted, every symphony that was ever played, and every dinner that was ever cooked was the child of someone's thinking.

So it is with a happy life.

Now we're back at the same question: *How do I set a goal for something as intangible as inner peace and happiness?*

The answer: *Think about it!*

Think about the kind of person you want to be. That in itself will take a lot of thought.

To begin with, you must think about two things: *where you are now* and *where you want to go*.

Well, where are you?

Who knows? Only you, of course. You might be on the verge of suicide. Or you might be a fairly happy person that gets down in the dumps now and then—nothing worse than that.

Suppose that's you.

Suppose you are somewhat like the widow who came to me for help last summer.

This woman had one married daughter and a son in college. She had a good job and no money problems. She was attractive, outgoing, a good talker, and well dressed. She appeared to be as happy as most people I talk to. Yet she explained that she felt spiritually stifled and lost.

This is what she said: "I used to be a happy person. But lately I've begun to feel burned out. I get despondent and down in the dumps for no reason. I live alone, but I don't think that's my problem. My husband died six years ago, and I have adjusted to that.

"When I get up each morning, I try to count my blessings. I tell myself how much better off I am than most people in the world. I run through the list. My children are doing well. No problems there. My home is paid for. I have a good job. My health is probably above the average. I live in America. By the time I leave for work, I feel pretty good.

"But when I get around people and hear them talk, I begin to get gloomy. I find myself joining in conversations about the uncertainty of the national economy and my own job security, about crime in the streets and drugs in our schools, about the danger from the nuclear bomb and acid rain and AIDS. I could go on and on. By the end of the day, I'm nothing but a worrywart. I know those things can't be ignored. But what can I do to keep them from depressing me? How do I put some good cheer back into my life? I want to get straightened out."

And so we chatted. We outlined the steps that would lead to the fulfillment she was seeking.

She had already taken the first step. She had made up her mind to do something about it. That's why she had come to talk to me.

So, with just a little help, she set her goal. "I want to become a cheerful person," she said, "I want to spread sunshine and gladness everywhere I go."

We discussed the power of thinking, and I told her about the little boy who climbed the magnolia tree so he could look out for pirates. I suggested that she climb to the top of her own magnolia tree and look toward the horizon and think about her goal.

"I'll do that," she said. "I promise. I'll start right now. But how do I reach my goal? Certainly there is more to reaching a goal than merely thinking about it. But how do I get there?"

She was right, of course.

And that brings us back to you.

It's time for you to take Step Number Two.

It's time for you to decide *where you want to go—to set your goals.*

It's time to establish your **sense of purpose**, so:

Do It!

Step Number Three

Now that you know *where* you are going, *how do you get there?*

Setting your big goal has given you a sense of purpose. Never let a day go by without thinking about your goal—*where you are going.*

One thing is certain. You can't get there merely by sitting and thinking about it. You've got to move. And before you move, before you back out of your driveway, you'd better know how to get where you are going.

Step Number Three shows you how to find your way. It calls for you to develop a **sense of direction**.

Remember the airline pilot? What do you think he had in his briefcase? Maps! Charts! Not the kind you pick up in a filling station, either. His charts are so detailed and give so much information that he was required to take a special course to learn to read them. And no matter how many times he flies over a course, he never leaves the airport without them.

Before he takes off, he files a detailed flight plan. He and his crew and traffic controllers at the points of departure and arrival will know where he is supposed to be at any given minute.

He knows exactly where he is going and how and when he is going to get there.

If you were going to drive from Miami, Florida, to Portland, Oregon, you certainly would do a lot of planning. You would begin by getting an up-to-date road map. You'd study it to see which of the many routes seemed best. You might choose a scenic route, or you might want to drive on the interstate highways. You'd check the mileage—not only to check the total distance but to see how many miles you would drive each day. You would decide whether to make the trip as quickly as possible or to stop along the way to visit friends or certain places of interest.

You'd probably plan where you would stop each night. You might even call one of the motel chains and make reservations along the way.

You'd chat with friends about your trip, especially if you knew someone who'd traveled over the same route.

A fellow was chatting with a friend in front of the post office in a small town. "Where are you going on your vacation this year?" he asked.

"My wife and I are repairing to take a trip to Dallas," the friend said.

"I hate to correct your English," the first fellow said, "but the word is 'preparing,' not 'repairing.' Repairing means to fix something."

"Yes," his friend replied, "That's what I said. My wife and I are fixin' to take a trip to Dallas."

So, if you're *fixin'* to take a trip, whether to Dallas or Portland, you wouldn't leave your home without an up-to-date road map—a well-planned itinerary—a sense of direction.

The same principle holds true in your spiritual journey through life—in your search for happiness. You won't get there by *meandering* along the way. You must follow a carefully planned itinerary. Don't start until you know the way.

You might ask, "How do I set up a spiritual itinerary? It's easy for an automobile trip. All I do is study a map. But where do I find a spiritual road map? How can I find the way?"

The entire ministry of Jesus embraced that question and many scholars and theologians have dedicated their careers to searching for the answers. But just as you don't need a college education in cartography to read a simple road map, you don't need to study the total life and teachings of Jesus to find your sense of direction. This book aims only to *help* you find a path to follow and *the steps to take* that will lead you to a happier and more abundant life. To make the road clearer, we will point to a few highlights found in the great book of wisdom—the Bible.

Now, in reply to the question, "How can I find the way?" listen to the words of Jesus: **"I am the way, and the truth, and the life"** (John 14:6). The essence of his teachings about the *way* comes to us in his great Sermon on the Mount.

Let us look briefly at certain parts of his sermon. Let him point the way. Let him tell you how to live right. Let him help you lay out your spiritual itinerary—your sense of direction.

Jesus opened his sermon with a poem that gave some rules for finding happiness. We call them the Beatitudes. He described the sort of person who would get the most out of life. He said this person is a humble one, who understands how to put misfortune and sorrow in perspective. This person submits his will to the will of God and tries to think right and to live right. He is kind to his neighbor, and he seeks to live a life free of contention. All Jesus' beatitudes center around a person's relationship to other persons. Not once does he mention personal power or possessions as the key to happiness.

Because Jesus' words were spoken about two thousand years ago, some of the ancient language is often misunderstood. For example, Jesus said, "Blessed are the meek, for they shall inherit the earth" (Matthew 5:5). Today, the word "blessed" is translated "happy," and our word "meek" doesn't mean what Jesus meant.

Webster defines *meek* as "mild, not inclined to anger or resentment, easily imposed on, submissive." You might have to stretch your imagination to picture that sort of person as being very happy. Instead, we are inclined to poke fun at him. Jokesters and cartoonists call him "Mr. Milquetoast." He is pictured as having no more backbone than a jellyfish, a person without drive or push or ambition, someone who wears a half-frightened or hangdog look.

So who wants to be meek?

The people who made our country great were those who had get-up-and-go, who were aggressive, who possessed leadership. Those are the folks we want to emulate.

So, let's look at that word "meek" more carefully to see if we can understand what Jesus meant.

A quick check of the scriptures shows that this saying was not original with Jesus. He was quoting from The Psalms. Psalm 37:11 reads: "But the meek shall possess the land."

That was written hundreds of years before Jesus. We are looking at a saying that has come down to us over a period of perhaps 2,500 years.

We also find the word "meek" in Numbers 12:3: "Now the man Moses was very meek, more than all men that were on the face of the earth."

Moses, meek?

If Moses was meek, then you can change the modern definition of the word.

So, when Jesus says, "Happy are the meek," what sort of person is he urging you to become?

What sort of person was Moses—really?

Was he mild? "Fiery" probably would describe him better. Was he inclined to anger? Yes, he was. He became so enraged that he killed one of the pharaoh's guards.

Was he easily imposed on? Not so you would notice. Rather, he became so incensed at the treatment of the Hebrews that he organized them, led them out of Egypt, and established them as a great nation. He did that because he was able to impose his ideas on them.

Was he submissive? There you get a yes and no answer. He refused to be subservient and submissive to the pharaoh. But when God called him to leave his hideaway and return to Egypt and lead his people, he submitted his will to the will of God. He let God guide him in everything he did.

Was he patient? He had to be, to lead that confused and mixed-up crowd of former slaves for forty years and eventually to build them into a powerful nation.

He was fair, just, firm, and compassionate. If he had not been, his people would have ousted him. He was their ruler, their judge, their source of inspiration and assurance. He was a dynamic leader. He was the dominant figure of his age. History shows that he was a man of great wisdom and judgment. He had a rare understanding of the needs of humanity far ahead of his time. He certainly rates among the greatest men who ever lived.

"Happy are the meek . . . ?"

Yes! Jesus would want us to be meek if we are going to follow his way.

Jesus also explained that, in order to follow his way, you have to put your whole heart into your effort. You can never be happy trying to *live right* in a listless and lackadaisical manner. Jesus had a great talent for using colorful and striking language. This is the way he said it: "Blessed are those who hunger and thirst for righteousness, for they shall be satisfied" (Matthew 5:6).

That word *righteousness* bothers some people. It sounds like a *religious* word or a *Bible* word. But the dictionary says it means "meeting the standards of what is right and just."

In modern language, Jesus is saying: Happy are they who seek the right way to live as urgently as they would yearn for food and water.

A less eloquent speaker might have said, "To be happy, you must do what's right."

But Jesus made a stronger point than that. When he said, "hunger and thirst," he was talking about something his audience understood. They lived in a land where food and water were scarce. They knew what it meant to hunger and thirst.

Have you ever been hungry? I'm not talking about the normal hungry feeling that comes at six o'clock in the evening. I'm talking about real hunger. Maybe I should have said, "Have you ever suffered from hunger?"

I know the feeling—in a mild way. I've never been anywhere near starving. But I thought I was. Last year I went on a diet to lose twenty pounds. Torture! Pure torture! I had difficulty concentrating on my work. All I could think about was food. On several occasions I wandered into the kitchen to stare into the refrigerator at all the food the rest of the household could enjoy but that was off limits to me. That didn't help. It was like beating myself over the head with a rubber hose.

Thirst hits you even harder. Experts in the field of nutrition say a person might live for days or even weeks without food. But sometimes in the desert, even half a day without water can be fatal.

Jesus said if you yearn for righteousness, the right way to live, like a hungry and thirsty person, you will be rewarded. You will be satisfied. Happiness will come with the same indescribable satisfaction that you get from that first sip of water or that first bite of food.

But this vivid word picture carried an even stronger point. Satisfaction is temporary. No matter how well you were filled today, the nagging call of hunger and thirst will return tomorrow.

So it is with your desire to live right. It must never leave you. Each morning as you face your new day, your desire to live *Jesus' way* should be as strong and as urgent as your need for food and drink.

Just as you don't let anything keep you from your breakfast and your early cup of coffee, you must let nothing divert you from your sense of purpose. You must let nothing sidetrack you from your sense of direction.

Don't be like the man who said to himself one Sunday after church, "This week I'm going to spend two hours studying next week's Sunday school lesson." Even though he meant well, and even though he put his Bible on the table next to his easy chair, his habit of procrastination overpowered his good intentions.

Come Saturday morning, he again said to himself, "This afternoon, without fail, I'm going to spend two hours reading tomorrow's lesson." But he didn't do it.

Oh, he had an excuse. It went something like this: "I was all set to work on that lesson when my attention was drawn to two great religious institutions as they met in a great cooperative venture. And that took all of my time." What he should have said was that he spent all Saturday afternoon watching a football game on television between Texas Christian University and Southern Methodist University!

When Jesus talked about his *way*, he had a lot to say about attitude and personal behavior.

He said that you should set an example in your community.

You are the light of the world. A city set on a hill cannot be hid. Nor do men light a lamp and put it under a bushel, but on a stand, and it gives light to all in the house. Let your light so shine before men, that they may see your good works and give glory to your Father who is in heaven (Matthew 5:14).

Jesus went on to point out that your good works should speak for themselves and that you shouldn't go around bragging about what you have done.

This is the way he said it:

Thus, when you give alms, sound no trumpet before you, as the hypocrites do in the synagogues and in the streets, that they may be praised by men. Truly, I say to you, they have received their reward. But when you give alms, do not let your left hand know what your right hand is doing, so that your alms may be in secret; and your Father who sees in secret will reward you (Matthew 6:2).

Jesus said, too, that when you are dealing with others, you will feel better if you add mercy to fairness and justice. He said, "Blessed are the merciful, for they shall obtain mercy" (Matthew 5:7).

Mercy needs special attention here because it is so easily misunderstood. Jesus talked about it because it is something rather special—and difficult to grant.

Ask a few friends about mercy, and you may get a strange response or two. "We believe in mercy," they may say. "We give to the Red Cross, the Salvation Army, the United Way, and the health drives. Our mercy is well organized too. In fact, we don't give it a second thought."

They would be right. They haven't thought about it. You don't show mercy when you give the Goodwill a dress that fit you before you gained that extra fifteen pounds or a suit of clothes that has been out of style for eight years.

The dictionary defines *mercy* as "kind and compassionate treatment of an offender, enemy, prisoner, or other person in one's power; clemency; a disposition to be kind and forgiving."

A classic description of justice and mercy is found in Shakespeare's *Merchant of Venice*. Portia, speaking to Shylock, says:

> The quality of mercy is not strain'd
> It droppeth as the gentle rain from heaven
> Upon the place beneath. It is twice bless'd;
> It blesseth him that gives and him that takes. . . .
> It is an attribute to God himself;
> And earthly power doth then show likest God's,
> When mercy seasons justice.

You can be merciful only when you *sit in judgment and have the power to act.*

Now you see why Jesus thought it was so important.

Let's call on your imagination to see how mercy might work, or might not, in a couple of cases.

A man was arrested for stealing a dozen or more chickens. Winter had set in, and there was a bit of snow on the ground. He was out of work, and his family was hungry. He had been driven to his act by poverty and what he considered necessity.

You read about his case in the newspaper, and you feel sorry for him. You can understand his plight. You pity him. And even though you might think that he should be forgiven, you can't show him any mercy. That's a matter for the courts to decide.

However, the situation is different if those were your chickens. In that case, the chicken thief's point of view might be harder for you to understand. Your pity might not be so forthcoming. And in the end, you might not be so anxious to see *justice seasoned with mercy.*

Now for another example.

Your brother-in-law borrows your new power mower that you have used only once. He mows his lawn that afternoon and leaves it outdoors beside the garage. It rains that night, and the next, and the next. After a week, when he hasn't bothered to return it, you drive by his house and pick it up. And right then you form a judgment—never again will you lend him *anything*.

When you get the mower home, you find that it won't start because he has used the wrong kind of gasoline in it. Besides, it has a broken blade.

Now you're boiling.

But your brother-in-law is a bit sheepish about the situation and says he's sorry and will pay to have it fixed. So you take it by the repair shop and tell the man to fix it. "I want it rebuilt just like new," you say, "I don't care what it costs because someone else is paying for it."

This is where understanding and justice and mercy come in. The fair thing would be to let him pay for it. You might even be justified in telling him he couldn't borrow it again.

But look how mercy might work. When your brother-in-law comes around to pay up, you refuse to take his money. Besides that, you say to him, "Forget it. It runs like new. No problem. Next time you need it, you're welcome to it."

Then, when he does come around to borrow it, you help him lift it into the back of his station wagon.

That's showing mercy. (I don't think I could do it.)

So, when you add *mercy* to your personal attributes, you have marked another landmark in your sense of direction.

Jesus says, "I am the way." You have listened to him as he points the way. And you have heard him describe the personal traits you will take there.

At this point, you may ask an age-old question. "Once I begin to follow his teachings—to follow *his way*—I'll live happily ever after. Is that the way it is?"

No!

That is the way fairy tales end.

But that is not the way life really is.

That is a fair question, however. Presumably, his disciples asked Jesus a similar question following his Sermon on the Mount.

Jesus answered it this way:

Every one then who hears these words of mine and does them will be like a wise man who built his house upon the rock; and the rain fell, and the floods came, and the winds blew and beat upon that house, but it did not fall, because it had been founded on the rock. And every one who hears these words of mine and does not do them will be like a foolish man who built his house upon the sand; and the rain fell, and the floods came, and the winds blew and beat against that house, and it fell; and great was the fall of it (Matthew 7:24).

Living according to *his way*, Jesus said, does not mean you will have a trouble-free life. But it does guarantee that you will be able to stand up against any of the evil forces that might seek to destroy you. He describes those evil forces as the rain and the floods and the winds.

Earlier in the sermon, Jesus explained that God treated his children fairly and impartially in that regard. "For he makes his sun rise on the evil and on the good," Jesus said, "and sends rain on the just and the unjust" (Matthew 5:45).

When Jesus speaks about the Christian attributes that will help you travel *his way*, he is talking about the foundation stones of character. As in all of his parables, his picture of the house built on the rock was carefully chosen.

Like a house, your character will stand against evil only if you build well, with the best materials available, and only if you anchor it securely on a solid moral foundation.

Let's follow Jesus' analogy a bit further. Building character *is* like building a house. You can't build either one overnight. You build your house brick by brick, board by board, one at a time. You form your character bit by bit too. Every time, every day, that you decide anything—when you decide between right and wrong—you add to your character. You either strengthen it or weaken it.

There's one big difference, however, between building physical houses and building character. When you build a house, you can call on outside help: an architect, a contractor, bricklayers, plumbers, painters, electricians, and so on.

But building character is a do-it-yourself project. When you build character, you serve as your own architect and contractor. You alone will decide whether or not your house is going to be a joy to live in and a shining tribute to the glory of God or a miserable hovel that will add to the spiritual slums of the world. And you alone will build it.

As you select the materials that go into your structure, you have two great advantages. The highest quality material doesn't cost any more than the shabbiest, and there is plenty of it available.

On the other hand, you won't have handy a building inspector standing there to help you. Not only that, the purveyors of the sleazy material will be falling over each other to sell you their products.

It's not easy to build a strong Christian character in today's chaotic world.

Picture this scene.

You have chosen for your foundation the strongest, most durable, and most reliable material on earth—faith. That's bedrock stuff. You know you can't lay the first brick without an abundant supply of it. And you have plenty on hand as you arrive at your building site the first morning.

When you get there, you find a long, black limousine parked on the site and a crew of men unloading a truck. A distinguished-looking man gets out of the limousine as you drive up. He looks prosperous, and he's one of the friendliest fellows you've ever met. He introduces himself as a public relations man and says something like this: "I'm head of a new company that has just opened up for business in town, and we want to build your house for you. We have a proposition that you can't turn down. I'm so sure that you'll accept that I already have my men unloading the first truck full of material."

"Wait a minute," you say, "I didn't hire you."

"I know, my friend," he says, "But you haven't heard my proposition. With a lifetime of experience behind me, I'll supervise the job myself. And there won't be any charge for time or materials. In other words, son, I'm going to build your new house for free. Free, do you hear? Free!"

"Why would you do that?" you ask.

"I'll tell you why, my friend," the fellow says, "You are one of the leaders in this community. When you have built this house and are living in it, we can point to you with pride and tell the world that you are one of our best customers. You are a man of influence. People look up to you. We're not dumb. Once we build for you, our firm will have a reputation of respectability, reliability, and integrity. We'll have all the business we can handle. It's nothing but public relations, son, public relations. And you can't turn it down."

While you stand there dumbfounded, he starts talking again before you have time to say anything.

"We've already gone to work. As soon as my men unload that truck, they're going to haul away that pile of faith that you were going to use for your foundation. Whoever told you that faith was good stuff was crazy. Why, man, you see it crumbling all over the country. Nobody depends on it anymore.

"That material that my men are unloading is the latest thing—skepticism. With the nuclear arms race, the rising crime rate, millions of kids being abused, everybody taking drugs, and half the married folks getting divorced, can't you see that you'd better look at the world the way it really is? Faith? Bunk! If you don't look at the world with skepticism, you're a sure loser, son."

"Who are you, anyway? What's your name?" you ask.

"Never mind my name," he will say, "You just leave this job to me. You can leave the construction site and go back home and relax. Fix yourself a drink and watch the football game on television. Go play golf, or go to the beach. Don't worry about anything. Then, one day I'll knock on your door and tell you that your house is finished. You don't need to know my name. But, I'll tell you one thing: I belong to a big conglomerate!"

He didn't tell you his name or the name of his organization—but I will. His name is Evil. His organization is the alliance of sin and degradation and hopelessness.

Because your faith is strong, you drive him away. But he'll be back. He'll keep delivering his inferior material to your house when you aren't looking. He'll send truckloads of concrete that will crumble and turn to sand when it rains. He'll send truck after truck of green lumber full of knotholes.

Build well. Begin with a solid foundation of faith because, sooner or later, your house will be tested.

So it is as you take Step Number Three. No matter how well you plan, and how carefully you navigate, you will be liable to the same hazards that face everyone else. But if you plan well and build well, no storm can defeat you.

Step Number One started you toward a fuller and more abundant life.

When you took Step Number Two, you gave yourself a goal—a sense of purpose.

Step Number Three says that, in order to fulfill your *purpose*, to reach your goal, you must figure out a way to get there. You must have a plan. You must give yourself a sense of direction.

Now is the time to

Do It!

Step Number Four

Let's see where you are.

Look at the steps you have taken.

1. You decided to take a trip.
2. You selected a destination.
3. You figured out how to get there.

Now you've come to Step Number Four. It's time to get ready for the trip.

Think again how you would prepare for your trip from Florida to Oregon. After you had charted your itinerary, you would get on with the rest of your plans.

You would make sure that you had enough cash for your day-to-day needs. Maybe you would even get some traveler's checks. If you planned to use your credit cards along the way, you'd double-check to be sure you had them and that they had not expired.

And finally, before you dared to hit the road, you'd get your car checked over. You'd give that high priority.

You would take it into a service station and tell the man you were getting ready to take it on a six thousand mile trip.

"Check everything," you would say, "Then give me a complete tuneup."

You'd even mention some things you wanted him to check, just to make sure he didn't miss anything. You'd tell him to put in new spark plugs and new filters and to check all the belts—fan belt, alternator belts, air-conditioner belts, and any others he might find under the hood. "And check all of the hoses," you would say. "Don't let me get caught in the middle of some lonely road with a broken radiator hose."

You would tell him: "Change the oil, check the transmission, and give me a good grease job. And don't forget to put fluid in my windshield washer bottle. And check the air in my tires. And be sure to check the brakes and turn signals."

If the service station manager is sharp, he would get into the spirit of things himself. He might say: "That's beautiful country you're going to visit. And you'll be driving through some of the most scenic parts of the United States. We'll put your car in first-class shape; you don't want any delays or trouble along the way.

"And speaking about trouble, you've got 35,000 miles on those tires. You probably would be able to get to Oregon and back with no problem, since the roads are good. But why not be on the safe side and let me put on a new set of radials? You'll need them when you get home, anyway. Why not do it now? And the peace of mind isn't going to cost you that much more money."

You'd say, "Go ahead."

Then, when you picked up your car, you would check the list of things he said he did to it. "Are you sure we didn't miss anything?" you'd ask.

He would run through the list. "I took out your spark plugs and put in special heavy-duty plugs. You'll see a lot of difference. You'll get better mileage, and you'll have quicker pickup. Your old plugs were burned out and eaten away to the point where I didn't see how your car could run at all.

"Then I tore out all of those old hoses, like you said. Man, you've been lucky! The main hose to your radiator just came to pieces in my hand when I started to take it off. Any day it was ready to go. I did the same with all the belts, just like you told me. And I put in new oil and a new filter.

"Driving around town like you do, you'd be surprised what filth and dirt get into your car's system. You sure did need a checkup! But you're all set now. Clean and pure inside, with all new stuff.

"And with those new radials you put on, you'll be able to take any kind of roads you'll run into along the way. Up and down the hills with no trouble. Even the weather won't bother you. You're set for a good, safe, smooth trip.

"I think we got everything," he'd say, "But just to make things run a little better, let me put a can of special additive in your gas tank. It's called GHPP. It adds extra pep to your motor. It makes it run smoother. I'm putting a couple of extra cans in your trunk in case your car overheats going over some of those mountains out west. If you get into trouble, just use some of that GHPP, and away you'll go."

That's how you would get ready for your cross-country trip from Florida to Oregon. That was easy.

But what about your *spiritual trip* from a dull and often depressed and melancholy existence to that exciting new state of living filled with joy and happiness?

Once again, the principle is the same.

And once again, you look to the Bible and to the words of Jesus for guidance.

"Blessed are the pure in heart," he says, **"for they shall see God."** (Matthew 5:8).

Jesus says you must have a pure heart, a clean heart, if you hope to find happiness. He says the person who thinks pure thoughts will be traveling the right way.

What kind of thinking is he talking about? What are *pure* thoughts? Pure thoughts may be contrasted with impure thoughts, just as pure water may be contrasted with polluted water. Clean, usable thinking is the opposite of thinking that is so filled with waste and extraneous matter that it actually poisons our mental ecology.

Jesus is pointing to that old rule: **If you think good thoughts, you'll have a good day; if you think bad thoughts, you'll have a bad day.**

That makes sense. If happiness is what you are, if happiness is born in your mind, if it comes from the way you think, then to be happy **you must first think happy thoughts**.

When you're talking to a happy person, you're talking to someone who is thinking *right*—someone, according to everyday slang, *who has his head on straight.*

There's nothing mysterious about that. It's obvious. It makes sense.

It's also obvious that if you are depressed and blue and down in the dumps and worried all the time, *something is wrong with the way you are thinking*.

So Step Number Four calls for you to check up on your way of thinking and to make a few changes.

This is the hardest step to take!

It's hard because making changes is hard.

Scholars and philosophers have been talking about the problems of change since the dawn of history.

Our libraries are full of books and essays and quotations about change from the world's great thinkers.

Twenty-five hundred years ago, Euripides said, "All is change." And four hundred years ago, Richard Hooker said, "Change is not made without inconvenience, even from worse to better."

President Kennedy talked about the importance of change. He said. "Change is the law of life. And those who look only to the past or present are certain to miss the future."

In spite of what anyone says, people hate change.

Maybe part of this resistance comes from fear of the unknown, or maybe in some cases people just cannot break an old habit.

You can see this rebellion against change all around you.

Take the little two-year-old who has been sleeping for a year under his Peter Rabbit blanket. Change it one day for a plain brown blanket, and watch his reaction. There's no way to predict what he'll say or do. He might sulk, have nightmares, cry, or not be able to sleep. Who knows what a two-year-old will do? But one thing you can count on—he'll miss his Peter Rabbit blanket, and he won't be happy.

Later, when he goes to school, he won't like changing teachers, or classrooms, or even schools.

When he's grown, he will still resist change. He will hate to give up an old sports jacket, change his favorite putter, or change his political party.

Enough talk about change.

Step Number Four toward happiness calls for you to make some changes, the hardest kind of changes—changes in your way of thinking.

But once you do it, the rest is easy.

Before you set out to change your way of thinking, look carefully at the part that needs changing. Take a *thought inventory*. What bad thoughts do you find? What are you going to quit thinking about? What good thoughts do you have? Surely, you have a few good thoughts. You don't need to change everything.

So, before you start on your trip to happiness, why not approach this step exactly the way you would begin your trip from Florida to Oregon?

Run a checklist before you start.

First, do you have *spiritual money in the bank*? For this trip, you need a desire to get there. You need the ability to make decisions. You need faith in yourself and the determination to reach your destination.

Do you have it? The answer is an obvious *yes*. Otherwise you would not have come this far. You would not be getting ready to take this next step.

Next, why not do the same thing with your mind that you would do with your car?

Get a spiritual checkup. See where you are and what you need to make your life run at full speed.

Get a mental oil change. Drain out the old lubricant that has become contaminated with negative thinking, and replace it with something clean and fresh that can accept new, positive thoughts.

Put in the new emotional spark plugs, and throw the old set in the trash can. Give your spiritual motor new energy and a quicker response to new ideas.

You'll notice this is a cleanup job, a renewal project. You can't merely drain your oil; you must replace it with new oil. You can't remove the old spark plugs and expect your engine to continue to run. You'll have to install new plugs.

So it is with your mind. It's not good enough to remove your useless and undesirable thoughts. You must replace them.

Your task is to substitute beneficial thoughts for harmful ones.

Here's the way to get started. Make a list of your bad thoughts and another list of your good thoughts. List everything. Be honest with yourself. On a clean sheet of paper, make three blank columns of equal width by drawing two lines from top to bottom.

In the left column, list any personal traits that you think create problems and unhappiness for you. Write down all the emotional trash you think may be contaminating your thinking—that cause you trouble. Examples are pride, despair, gloom, pessimism, and a long list of others.

In the center column, opposite each of these words, write the word that describes the quality that should replace it.

Examples: humility in place of pride; hope to replace despair; optimism to take the place of pessimism; and cheerfulness in place of gloom.

In the right-hand column, grade yourself with regard to the quality in the middle column. Use any system you like: A, B, C, D, or 1 to 10, or 1 to 100. Just so you understand it yourself. Example: Take *gloom*. Your aim is to change the gloom in your system into *cheerfulness*. If you are cheerful and never have any gloomy moments, give yourself a top grade, an A or a 10.

This exercise will help you look inside yourself. You are trying to see yourself as others see you.

When you finish this study, you will know exactly what sort of changes you'll have to make in your thinking. Nobody else is going to read this list, so you can be 100 percent honest. That's important.

We'll work together on this, to see how it goes and to stimulate your thinking. Let's begin by starting with the attribute that probably causes as much unhappiness as most of the others together: pride! Opposite pride write humility.

Before you grade yourself on this one, study it carefully.

Pride heads the list of the seven deadly sins. On the other hand, some dictionary definitions make it sound worthy and acceptable. For example: "(1) A sense of one's own proper dignity; self-respect. (2) Pleasure or satisfaction taken in one's work, achievement, or possessions. (3) A cause or source of pride."

But look at "(4) An excessively high opinion of oneself; conceit; arrogance." That's the attitude mentioned in the book of Proverbs: "Pride goes before destruction, and a haughty spirit before a fall" (16:18).

Pride is so evil and dangerous because it is so subtle. It creeps up on you.

You might compare it to phenobarbital. When prescribed by a physician, and taken according to directions, phenobarbital can be helpful. On the other hand, it can be addictive, and an overdose can lead to a tragedy.

Pride is like that.

Civic pride can lead to a better government, or to city beautification or the support of a successful football team. A business person might take pride in her or his work. A young woman might take great pains with her personal appearance because of pride. A retired man might take pride in his garden.

In those cases, pride can be beneficial.

But what happens when pride becomes addictive?

An overdose of civic pride could lead to a riot on a football field. A business person who lets pride become addictive may become boastful and overbearing and arrogant. A young woman could become so puffed up about her good looks that she could eventually lose all her friends. A gardener could be in trouble if his whole life depended on a good crop of vegetables or flowers.

Pride can be a sort of spiritual cancer. It can spread and grow until it consumes and destroys a person. It can take many forms.

You see the pride of being right—self-righteousness—all around you, every day. Self-righteous people are arrogant in their judgments, uncharitable with those who differ from them, and unwilling to listen to anyone. Generally, they are unhappy with the world and everything in it.

Jesus had a word to say about the self-righteous. He told the story about the Pharisee and the publican to illustrate his point.

> The Pharisee stood and prayed thus with himself, "God, I thank thee that I am not like other men, extortioners, unjust, adulterers, or even like this tax collector. I fast twice a week, I give tithes of all that I get." But the tax collector, standing far off, would not even lift up his eyes to heaven, but beat his breast, saying, "God, be merciful to me a sinner." I tell you, this man went down to his house justified rather than the other; for everyone who exalts himself will be humbled, but he who humbles himself will be exalted (Luke 18:11).

Then there are those who take pride in their personal possessions: their clothes, their home, their new yacht, their new car, their jewelry.

Some are proud of their heritage—who they are. Or rather, who their forebears were. They want everyone to know they are members of one of the "first families." Think of all the friends they never get to know because pride keeps them from mixing with ordinary people.

Humility stands as the opposite of pride. To show the absurdity of pride, a story is told of a monk in a small monastery in the California mountains. One day he was talking with a visitor who had stopped by. "We're just a small order," the monk said, "We don't operate a winery, a hospital, or even a roadside hostel. We're very poor. Our only mark in the world is our humility. I would say we're the humblest order of monks in all of California. And knowing that makes us mighty proud."

How far can pride drag a person? It can lure him to seek honor and glory and public applause. It can take him to the place where he thinks he did everything by himself. He thinks he is self-sufficient and is responsible for his own good fortune. He forgets the part God played in his destiny. And any chance he had for happiness is destroyed—by pride.

However, this is not true of the humble person who has opened his heart to God. He seeks no honor or glory. He doesn't need the spotlight. Having emptied his heart of selfish thoughts, he has replaced them with the wonderful and exciting thoughts of others. He has freed himself from the mental isolation that comes to the person who is self-centered and self-righteous.

So, put *pride* on your list of things to kill, and mark down humility to take its place. Let this be your first aim as you take Step Number Four.

Go now to another word: *despair*.

Did you ever suffer from despair? Do things get so bad sometimes that you feel like giving up? That's a good place to start because that feeling creeps up on most of us at one time or another.

That's a horrible word: *despair*. But put it at the top of the page on your left.

Then, in the center column, write one of the greatest words in the English language—the word that stands as the everlasting symbol of the teachings of Jesus. Write the word *hope*.

Jesus came as the *hope* of the world. Our first step toward creating a pure heart—a clear mind—is to get rid of *despair* and to replace it with *hope*.

You could hardly start with a better word. Because *hope* can utterly destroy *despair*.

When hope is alive and strong, all things are alive and strong. Hope is Daniel standing in the lions' den. Hope is David fleeing from his enemies but looking forward to the day when he would be king of Israel. David never lost hope. He recognized the part it played in his life.

We mustn't become confused about *hope*. A woman was on board ship and was rather sick. The steward was trying to comfort her and said, "You'll be all right. Remember, no one has ever died of seasickness."

"Oh," she said, "I'm sorry to hear that. It's only been the hope of dying that's kept me alive."

Every great project accomplished by the human race began with hope. Hope for something better. Some long-forgotten sage once said, "We all hope for the best, and if we get it we hope for something better." Even when the hour seems darkest, there are no hopeless situations; there are only people who have grown hopeless about them.

Remember, too, that it was *hope for greater happiness* that has brought you to *Step Number Four*.

Now, back to that sheet of paper. How did you grade yourself?

Let's go again. Write these two words: *pessimistic* in the left column; *optimistic* in the right.

Which are you? These words describe your general attitude toward everyday happenings. They describe how you look at things that are going on around you.

This is important because pessimism will make your spiritual motor knock and lose power on the hills. Optimism will keep it running smoothly even during a snowstorm.

People like to joke about optimists and pessimists. One man described an optimist as a fellow who was trying to raise

Easter lilies, half a dozen ducks, two cats, a dog, a vegetable garden, and three boys on half an acre of land.

A pessimist is a fellow who sits and worries when everything is all right because he knows that if he worries when things are all right, he will worry more when things get worse; and he knows that because things are so good now, they will get worse.

So much for making fun of optimists and pessimists.

The real picture is more serious. A pessimist looks at the dark side of everything. Maybe he doesn't mean any harm; he just can't help himself. If you accused him of being a pessimist or a negative thinker, he would deny it. But let's listen to a pessimist for a few minutes.

A woman buys a gift for a friend—a pair of gloves. As she puts them in the mail, she says, "She probably won't like the color," or "I hope she'll wear them, but I'll bet they don't fit," or "I bought long gloves, and I have a feeling she likes short gloves." And on and on.

Two men are watching a football game on television. The team they are rooting for has the ball on the four-yard line with "goal to go." "Watch them fumble," the pessimist says. The optimist sits on the edge of his chair, enjoying the moment, shouting, "Go! Go! Go!"

The Labor Day picnic? "I'll bet it will be rained out," the pessimist says, "We've had seven good years in a row. No problem with the weather. We're long past due. I'll bet we get it this year."

This is an important trait to check on, for if you look on everything with a pessimistic eye, you'll become known as a *sourpuss*. You'll also be wasting an opportunity to think a happy thought every time you let that ugly thought creep in.

Instead of worrying about the gloves pleasing her friend, that woman should have said to herself, "I spent an hour picking out the gloves that I think she will like. But, to make sure, I'll put a note in the box telling her where she can exchange them if they don't fit. I know she'll appreciate the thought behind the gift."

What about the Labor Day picnic? "This will probably be another good one," the optimist says, "It will be eight in a row. That's because I always take my raincoat. I leave it in the back seat of the car. If I ever forget to take it, that's the day it will rain."

That's silly thinking, of course. But it's no sillier than thinking that this is the year it will rain. Besides, it turns a sour thought into a happy thought.

So much for looking on the bright side of things.

Up to now you have looked at pride and despair and pessimism, and you have seen that they can clutter up a pure heart and help generate all sorts of unhappy thinking. And you have seen what healthy attributes you must put in their place: humility, hope, and optimism.

As you continue your spiritual checkup, you will make your own list of qualities that need study and change. But to give you a further push in that direction, here are a few you may want to think about.

If you find any of these in your mental inventory, you will want to change: suspicion into trust; hypocrisy into sincerity; jealousy into understanding; ugliness into beauty; discourtesy into courtesy; revenge into forgiveness; vanity into modesty;

enmity into friendliness; hatred into love; and a dozen more such changes that you can identify.

There you are!

As in getting ready for a trip across the United States, you have prepared yourself for a journey to a happier and more fulfilling life.

You've made a mental tuneup, and you're ready to go.

"Wait a minute," you might say, "You talked about emotional spark plugs, and a mental oil change, but what about that can of GHPP? You forgot about that."

You're right. I almost forgot to mention that. The service station man said that was the stuff that would give you extra power when you need it. He said to use it when you think you can't get over the next mountain. He said it would restore your strength and vigor when things aren't going well. He certainly knew what he was talking about.

He called it GHPP.

That stands for *God's Hidden Power—Prayer*.

And that's what you'll find out about in Step Number Five.

But right now, you're ready to start on Step Number Four.

Do It!

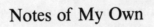

Notes of My Own

Step Number Five

"Hey, wait a minute," you are going to say, "Hold the phone. Don't move so fast. I haven't even done Step Number Four."

You are right!

You'll never *finish* Step Number Four.

Because Step Number Four is about change.

Change never rests. It never ends. It keeps moving. It must go on and on from day to day—all the time.

Step Number Four showed how to use change to your advantage. It gave you some practical suggestions for changing your unhappy thinking into happy thinking.

Change! You see it all around you—every day. New streets and buildings keep our cities moving ahead. At the same time, some parts of the city decay, and rot, and fall into disrepair.

Change! In government you witness constant change. Only in some rare cases, in this country, will you find the present leadership in power ten years from now.

Change! It touches you every day. Your job. Your friends. Your car. Even your children change. Several years ago a study showed that the average American family moved every seven years.

Change! Spring—summer—fall—winter! The changing of the seasons. This cycle means so much to some people that they travel hundreds of miles to see the leaves change color in the fall. Many northerners who retire and move to Florida complain that they miss the dramatic changes in the seasons.

Change! The idea that change is constantly going on around you is not new. It's easy to see and to understand that kind of change—physical change.

It's not always easy to see and understand spiritual change, personality change, a change in attitude—especially when you are looking at yourself. And that is what this book seeks to do: (1) to show that you can change—that you can change from an unhappy person to an extremely happy person, (2) to show what sort of changes you should make, and (3) how to make them.

Step Number Four explained how to determine what changes you need to make.

This new step, Step Number Five, tells you how to find the help and support you will need to make those changes.

You'll need help, make no mistake about that.

You will face two problems as you try to make those changes. First, you are not going to find it easy to reverse a pattern of thinking that has taken years to establish. To put it bluntly, it's hard for anyone to change when they are "set in their ways."

Second, you must constantly be on guard so you don't become careless and let your old habits return. That's what some people call "backsliding."

You can fall into that trap without knowing it. Suppose you have looked at yourself and have seen someone who is highly successful in business—a person recognized in the community for civic commitment. And suppose you have been overly proud of yourself.

Suppose you set out to change that pride into humility. Suppose you have even quit bragging about yourself, for example, and have quit talking about events in which you took a prominent part. Suppose you have begun to feel the difference in yourself and that you like the person you now are.

Then, bingo! You get up some morning and see your picture on page one of the business section of your newspaper, and before the day is over you have appeared on all three television stations as "Business Leader Named Citizen of the Year."

That's when you run the risk of stepping into that old trap: "It's hard to be humble when you're such a great person."

So, as you go about changing your way of thinking, you're going to need all the help you can find. And there is plenty of it around.

You just have to know where to look.

Again, let's look to the Bible for guidance.

Jesus gave us a great spiritual law that covers the situation. He said: **"Ask, and it will be given you; seek, and you will find; knock, and it will be opened to you"** (Matthew 7:7).

Some people refer to that as a "promise." I think it is more than that. I think Jesus was stating a spiritual law. He said if you do certain things in a certain way, then you will get certain definite results. He stated it as a simple truth.

When God created the universe, he designed it to operate in an orderly manner according to certain physical laws. They never change. They never vary. Sir Isaac Newton studied those laws. Einstein had more to say about them. Scientists and engineers were able to send men to the moon because they understood some of those laws and had learned to make use of them.

Just as scientists explain our physical laws, here we see Jesus stating a great spiritual law.

He is giving us the three pillars of success.

Prayer! Hard Work! Persistence!

You will notice that he listed the most important first—*prayer*.

Let's talk about prayer for a moment and see how it can help you on the road to happiness.

To begin with, prayer opens a direct line of communication with God. Properly used, it becomes an unlimited source of amazing power.

You cannot overestimate the power of prayer.

Jesus' disciples knew about it. They had traveled and worked with Jesus and had seen how he relied on prayer. They had seen him cure people with palsy and mental illness. They had been with him when he made the lame walk and the blind see, and even when he raised a man from the dead.

Their days with Jesus had been filled with wonderment. Yet when the opportunity came for them to ask him for a favor, a gift, they did not ask him to teach them to change water into wine or to feed five thousand people with a few loaves and fishes. They did not say, "Lord, teach us how to perform miracles." Instead, they said, "Lord, teach us to pray."

Jesus thought prayer was important. He prayed.

Most Christians believe in prayer. We are taught to pray as soon as we can walk and talk. Do you remember this prayer?

Now I lay me down to sleep.
I pray the Lord my soul to keep,
If I should die before I wake,
I pray the Lord my soul to take.

Following those lines, the little tot usually asks God to "Bless Mama and Papa and dear Aunt Sarah and. . . ." Those prayers are said with great faith and genuine fervor.

But as many people grow older, the realities of the world seem to dampen their faith and weaken their ardor for prayer. They lose the benefits of this great power because they don't recognize its importance or understand how to use it. So prayer ceases to be a part of their daily routine.

You will find others who do pray, but pray improperly. You sometimes hear them say, "I have tried it, but prayer just doesn't work for me." Like the woman mentioned earlier who prayed for the mountain to disappear, they don't really believe it will work. She might have said, "See! The mountain is still there. God didn't answer my prayer."

But God did answer her prayer. He said, "No!"

Why did he say, "No"?

Because she had asked for something that was against God's will. She had forgotten what Jesus told his disciples. He had said that when they prayed, they should remember to say, "Thy will be done."

She also had confused the physical world with the spiritual world. She didn't understand that prayer is a *spiritual* process and that the results of prayer are *spiritual*.

Many people, including devout Christians, make that same mistake. They ask for things that obviously are against God's will. The woman who prays for a new dress, or the man who asks for a new outboard motor for his boat, or the youngster who begs for a bicycle—all will be disappointed.

Why? Because those requests were made against God's will—against his rules.

God rules the world by a set of laws—physical and spiritual. They are strict. They are dependable and reliable because they are inflexible. God's judgment and understanding and love are perfect. God does not change his rules to *fit the situation*.

He does not treat his children like so many modern-day parents. For example, the father of a teenager may have a rule that says, "You can't use the car on any night following a sporting event."

Then comes the big homecoming game. The boy's girlfriend will reign as homecoming queen. This is something special. So the boy pleads with his father. "This will be the only time I will ever ask you. But Sue is the queen. I'm a senior, and this is my last year—my last chance. Blah, blah, blah." His prayer is long and loud and so earnest that his father gives in.

"Okay, my son," he says, "just this once. And be sure to be home by twelve o'clock."

You might be surprised how many parents give in to their children like that. And you might be surprised how many rotten, spoiled children there are in the world too.

Does God give in to our prayers like that?

No! Just plain *no*.

God doesn't bend his laws—his will—just because somebody begs him loudly enough.

Take the law of gravity. According to that law, if you drop a baseball, it will *fall* toward the Earth. And ten thousand prayers and ten thousand devout Christians will not persuade God to make it fall *up* instead of *down*.

The law of gravity is inflexible.

One thing is obvious. God isn't going to nullify the law of gravity just because you ask him to do so.

Since that is true, what did Jesus mean when he said, "Ask, and it will be given you" (Matthew 7:7)?

He's talking about requests that conform to God's rules—to his will.

He is saying that the power of prayer is reserved for spiritual matters. He meant that if you need spiritual help, all you need to do is ask for it.

This spiritual law is important to everyone who is trying to find a happier way of life.

As one man said, "It's hard to be humble when you are such a great man!" It's hard to replace despair with hope when the roots of despair are deeply seated. It's hard to be optimistic and cheerful when you stagger under the weight of personal tragedy.

This journey toward happiness can become difficult. And from time to time all of us need help.

Jesus said help is available—just for the asking.

The key, then, must lie in *what* to ask for.

You must also understand what *not* to ask for.

Let's pretend for a moment. Suppose someone has listed *revenge* as one of his poor traits, and suppose he is trying to develop a spirit of *forgiveness* to take its place. Suppose he gets up in the morning and says, "Lord, among other things today, make me forgive my old buddy that I have been trying to get even with for so long, because I want to be happy about everything."

Now, let's quit pretending. That fellow is not going to get far down the road with his plan for forgiveness. That wasn't much of a prayer to begin with. "Make me forgive my old buddy," he said, "because I want to be happy." He wanted God to do all the work. He wanted God to make him happy. If life were that simple, most of the problems of the human race would disappear overnight.

Yes, that fellow had asked for the wrong thing.

What should he have asked for?

He should have asked for God's *help*.

Help? What did he need God to help him do?

He needed God to help him with Step Number Four. He needed God to help him change his way of thinking.

Step Number Five shows him how to get God's help. Jesus said, "Ask, and it will be given you" (Matthew 7:7).

That man's prayer would have been answered if he had said something like this: "Lord, I need your help as I seek control of my thinking. Please help me as I search for understanding, and wisdom, and patience, and tolerance. Please help me as I seek ways to purge my mind of harmful and selfish thoughts and to replace them with beneficial and uplifting thoughts."

That's the kind of prayer Jesus is talking about when he said, "Ask, and it will be given you."

Prayer is the first part of this spiritual law. What comes next? Jesus said, "Seek, and you will find."

If you want wisdom and understanding and patience, and a hundred other great personal qualities, you must *seek* ways to develop these attributes. They are not going to be given to you on a silver platter. Remember, your prayer should be *help me find wisdom*, not *give me wisdom*. If you seek hard enough, you'll find what you are looking for. That is true. That's a spiritual law, just as inflexible as the law of gravity.

Seeking usually ends up as *hard work*.

For example, you may be a salesperson. Maybe you aren't doing very well and you need help. So you ask God to help you be a better salesperson. He'll do it. He'll do his part, if you do your part. His part is to strengthen your desire and your determination and your confidence. Your part is to study your product and to develop the proper attitude toward your work and all the people with whom you deal.

God will help you develop the right outlook, the right attitude, the right spirit—but you'll have to *seek* your business opportunities. You'll have to carry your own briefcase!

God will help you spiritually. He will help you control your thinking. But you must *seek*. You must do your share of the work.

On the other hand, if you don't learn to take charge of your thinking, you can easily drift into poor mental habits.

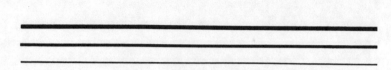

Call it *wrong thinking*. That leads to unhappiness and, in extreme cases, to what is generally called a nervous breakdown.

But once you learn to control your thinking, wonderful and sometimes strange things happen.

I have a friend who had a strange problem. He likes to watch football on television. He always watched a college game on Saturday, a professional game on Sunday, and never missed Monday night football.

His problem? He would get so intense over rooting for *his teams* that when one of them lost, he suffered. The rest of his day was ruined. When the score didn't come out to suit him on Monday night, he didn't sleep well.

My friend is well educated and a highly successful businessman. He also happens to be a Sunday school teacher.

He's cheerful. He's great at dinner meetings and conferences. He wears a smile everywhere he goes, and he speaks to everybody. And he always has something good to say about everything. You never fail to learn something when you are with him.

Once when we were visiting and chatting about all sorts of things, the subject of *right thinking* came up. We had talked many times about my six steps to happiness and how important it is to control your own thinking.

"Oh, man!" he said, "That's right. I almost let football get the best of me until I learned how to control my attitude toward it."

"That's a new one," I said, "You never mentioned that before. Tell me."

Then he explained how he used to become upset and tense and frustrated when the team he was pulling for lost.

I said, "Me too. It's silly, but it's true."

"Not me," he said, "Now I can watch a whole weekend full of football and enjoy every minute of it—no matter who wins."

"Even when your favorite team loses," I said.

"That's it," he said, "I don't have a favorite. I figure that any two teams that are good enough to get on television will play an interesting game. I never care who is playing."

"Oh," I said to him, "What do you do, pick a team to root for just as the game starts?"

"I don't watch football that way," he said. He went on to explain how he does watch the game. "As you know, I like to get things done. I like to see people succeed. I get a kick out of watching other people accomplish something. So when I apply my way of looking at life to a football game on television, I find myself always rooting for the team that has the ball.

"I enjoy seeing a quarterback throw a long pass and the ball caught for a touchdown. And I'm always pulling for the fellow who is trying to kick a field goal.

"You think about it. Let's say you're pulling for a favorite team, and they only get two touchdowns while the other team gets four. You have enjoyed the excitement of only two touchdowns. Four touchdowns that day have left you with a sick feeling. And all you got out of watching that game was about three hours of disappointment.

"Yes, I always pull for the team with the ball."

Millions of football fans around the world will disagree with my friend, of course. But he has found a *way of thinking* about football that brings him enjoyment.

That change in his *thinking pattern* didn't come accidentally. He had to *seek* for the answer.

This shows that you can adjust yourself to any pattern of thinking you wish.

Now let's go back and see how that would work for that man who asked God to make him forgive his old buddy.

He could have handled it by asking God to help him *understand* his old buddy's point of view. He could have asked for help in his search for a *wise* solution to his problem. He could have said, "Lord, after you have helped me understand his side and I have tried to make a wise decision, please help me use good *judgment* in dealing with my old buddy."

Then, knowing God was helping him, he could have gone to work. He might have discussed his problem with some of his friends in an effort to see his old buddy's point of view—to better understand both sides of the controversy. He might have turned to the Bible in his search for wisdom. With that approach, he would have been prepared to judge the matter in a new light. If he handled things that way, the chances are his desire for revenge would be completely erased.

So much then, for prayer and hard work. But what about that third part of this spiritual law: "Knock, and it will be opened to you" (Matthew 7:7)? Where does that come in?

Jesus was emphasizing what every wise person knows. The important doors to success don't open automatically like those at the airport or supermarket.

The automatic doors were designed to make it easy for people to go in and out with suitcases or bundles in their arms.

But the doorways in real life don't open that easily. They open the *old-fashioned way—you have to knock on them.*

Knocking means praying daily—not just on Sunday or when you are in trouble.

Knocking is an exercise in persistence. You can call it tenacity. You can call it perseverance. But whatever you call it, it's simply the determination to stick to a job, never to give up hope. One thing is certain—you can't succeed without it.

When you are standing in the rain at two o'clock in the morning, pounding on your friend's front door—you are putting your faith into action.

Oh, you know he's there. And you have faith in his friendship. But he's not going to open that door unless you bang on it loud enough to wake him up.

Winston Churchill, the man who led Great Britain to victory in World War II, knew the importance of persistence. In one of his stirring speeches, he said, "Never give up. Never, never, never give up."

One of the great examples of persistence comes from the legend of Robert Bruce, king of Scotland. The king was fighting a war with England and had lost six battles in a row. In full retreat, he was hiding from his enemies in a squalid hut. As he lay resting on a bed of hay, he watched a spider that was spinning a web on a rafter above his head.

Six times the little spider tried to swing itself from one beam to the other. Six times it failed. Then, on its seventh try, it reached the other beam.

Jumping to his feet, King Bruce cried, "For shame, to think that the king of Scotland has not the will to win as this lowly spider. I'll try again, and this time we'll drive the English out of this fair land." And of course, he did. He defeated the English at the battle of Bannockburn and later was recognized by Edward III as King Robert I.

A man with a sense of humor explains persistence this way: A television interviewer was talking to a man who was celebrating his hundredth birthday.

"To what do you attribute your long life," he asked the old man.

"Oh, I'm a golfer," the old fellow said, "I played eighteen holes of golf until I was eighty. Since then I have played nine holes a day. There's nothing like golf to keep a man going."

"That's interesting," the interviewer said, "But I had an uncle who played golf every day. He died when he was sixty-six. How do you account for that?"

"That was his own fault," the old man said, "He just didn't keep it up long enough."

And so it goes.

Now, back to the problem in Step Number Four: the task of cleaning your mind of impure thoughts and filling it with worthwhile thoughts, the difficulty of changing your thinking habits.

Yes, it's hard to change.

But once you have set your goal and have begun to work toward it, you can get plenty of help along the way.

Just remember what Jesus said: "Ask, and it will be given you; seek, and you will find; knock, and it will be opened to you" (Matthew 7:7).

Nothing, then, can defeat you in your search for happiness when you

Do It!

Step Number Six

Welcome to the *launch pad* of great joy!

Things are getting ready to happen.

But before you *blast off* toward a fuller and more abundant life, pause for a moment to check up.

Let's see how far you have come.

Up to this point, you have been preparing yourself for a *great adventure in living*.

The first five steps outlined a rigorous program of mental self-discipline.

You might call it a spiritual training schedule. It's as demanding as—and in many ways similar to—the physical fitness routine of a professional athlete.

The steps he must follow toward success are much the same as you are taking toward happiness. At some time or other he decided to "turn pro." If he wanted to be a quarterback, that became his main goal. To succeed, he had to think of all the skills he needed to develop in order to handle the job.

He not only had to learn football, he also had to study football strategy and the psychology of winning. Besides, he had to develop the qualities of leadership that would inspire his teammates to back him up on the field.

Then he had to go to work. He had to practice day in and day out—for two reasons. One, to keep from "getting rusty," and two, to constantly improve his proficiency.

Likewise, when you see a golfer drive a ball 250 yards down the center of the fairway, you can be sure she has spent hours and hours on the driving range. And if she expects to win any tournaments, she'll spend just as much time, or more, practicing putting.

What about the batter who hits a home run in the first game of the new season? That fellow had to be in top form. And he had not "kept in shape" by drinking beer and loafing in front of a television set during the off season, either. Some way or other, he had been practicing.

So it is with your spiritual development.

The first five steps have prepared you for the big game—for the trip to the moon. You have a sense of purpose—you know where you want to go. You have a sense of direction—you know how to get there. You have begun to rid yourself of the mental barriers that were in your way and have replaced them with vital and stimulating thoughts. And you have discovered that help is constantly at your elbow, waiting to be called on.

By now, you should be in good shape. You're ready for the big game. So, **get busy.** Start moving.

Again, you might say, "Wait a minute! What's all this about a big game? You say 'get busy.' Get busy doing what? You said happiness is a kind of thinking. I've been doing that, and I do feel better. And I'm sure that the more I think good thoughts, the easier it will become. But what's that got to do with doing anything? What am I supposed to do?"

Those are fair questions. And I'm sure they'll stimulate other questions. So, as we look at this important step toward a permanent *happiness plan* in your life, let's enjoy a bit of give-and-take about it.

First, your question, "What am I supposed to do?"

The answer to that is simple. You have been learning the strategy for happiness and have developed a powerhouse of energy. But the greatest powerhouse in the world doesn't accomplish anything until it is turned on—until the power is put to work.

Therefore, you'd better turn on the power. You had better get moving. *Because action is the key to happiness.* Watch out for that word *key.* Action itself isn't the whole answer. Action only opens the door to happiness.

What kind of action?

As in the first five steps, you can find your answer in the Bible. Again we listen to the words of Jesus himself: **"As you wish that men would do to you, do so to them"** (Luke 6:31).

Right away, you might start asking more questions: "Hey, that's the Golden Rule, 'Do unto others as you would have them do unto you.' You're nothing but a fraud. If that is the Sixth Step to Happiness, why didn't you say so in one paragraph? You could have said the secret to happiness is the Golden Rule. And you could have said it in one sentence. You didn't need to write a book. Where does the Golden Rule fit in?"

It fits in right here! To understand how it fits in, let's take a close look at it.

A great many people misunderstand the Golden Rule. At one time or another you may have heard someone speak of the Golden Rule in this fashion, "I make it a point to live by the Golden Rule. It's really the basis of my religion. I'm not a churchgoer anymore. I used to go, but I see too many hypocrites there. All that singing and praying doesn't help me any. Besides, I work six days a week, and Sunday is the only day I have to relax. I'm sure I'm just as good as a lot of people who go to church. Instead, I make it a point to live by the Golden Rule. I think it summarizes the entire teaching of Jesus. That's all of Christianity in a nutshell."

If you ever hear anyone say that, ask what he means. He will probably tell you that, no matter what comes up, he acts according to the Golden Rule. In a pious tone he may tell how the cashier in a restaurant gave him thirty-six cents too much change, how he called her attention to it and gave it back. Or when he drives through busy city traffic, he often lets another car go ahead of him. Or maybe he will tell you how he has made many business deals with only a handshake.

"Yes," he will say, patting himself on the back, "In everything I do, I act according to the Golden Rule."

Don't you believe it.

He is not *acting*. He's merely *reacting* to a situation. He may even follow the Golden Rule, but he uses it only as a pattern for reacting to something someone else has done. According to his interpretation, he might sit for weeks and never put the Golden Rule into use. He only dusts it off and looks at it when someone crosses his path.

If it didn't mean more than that, it never would have come down to us through twenty centuries.

Jesus wasn't telling you how to *respond* to someone else's action. He was saying you should *initiate* some action. Neither was he giving you a sugar-coated motto to recite on Sundays and to forget during the week.

When Jesus gave the world the Golden Rule, he was laying down a great spiritual law. Some Bible scholars even call it *the eleventh commandment.*

He uses one of the most powerful words in any language— *do.* "Get busy," he says, "Do something."

"Do what?" you might ask.

"It doesn't matter much what you do," he would say, "just so you do it for someone else. Be sure it's something you would like for someone to do for you."

If he were a modern Sunday school teacher, he might have written it on the blackboard like this:

"Do [*something helpful*]
for others [*anybody—even strangers*]
as [*right now*]
you would like them [*if you had your wish*]
to do for you."

"That's supposed to make me happy?" you ask.

Let's run a quick little test to see if it does.

Start with a sheet of paper like the one you used for Step Number Four. Draw a line down the center of the page. At the top of the left column, write the words *For Me* and at the top of the right, *For Others*. Think back over the past two or three weeks, and remember how you felt about various experiences, events, and happenings.

In the left column, list the occasions when someone did something for you—sent you a birthday card, took you to lunch, or perhaps gave you a book.

In the right column, list some of the things you did for someone else. Maybe you sent someone a birthday card, or took a friend to lunch, or gave someone a book.

Study that sheet carefully. The further back you go, the clearer the answer becomes. What you did for others brought you more lasting pleasure than the things that were done for you.

Of course, you didn't have to make that little comparison test. Jesus told us the same thing in so many words. "It is more blessed to give than to receive." (Acts 20:35). Think about it. You'll discover you *are* happier over what you do for someone than for something that is done for you.

Not that you were unhappy over something that someone did for you. Not at all. You may have been extremely happy. But when you put a part of yourself into an act, its effect is stronger and longer lasting.

For example, suppose you had a Sunday afternoon visit from your son and his wife and two children—a little boy of seven and his four-year-old sister. The children love you and like to visit you, so they brought you a big jar of jelly beans. "These are the kind of jelly beans the President likes," they said. You accepted the gift with great enthusiasm and gratitude and much hugging and kissing. They were so proud that they had selected a gift you liked. And even though you aren't much of a jelly bean fan, their thoughtfulness gave you a noticeable spiritual lift. That was a happy event, no question about it.

As grandparents are supposed to do, you had gifts for them too—a big beach ball for the boy and a picture book for the little girl. The book was one of those rub-and-smell books. That is, throughout the book there were spots that give off a special fragrance when you rub them—maybe a peppermint smell for a candy cane or a smell of pine for a Christmas tree.

The kids were elated. The boy headed for the backyard where he had plenty of room to play with his ball. The little girl insisted on climbing on your lap so you could read to her and she could rub-and-smell. She nearly wore you out because you went through that book over and over until your finger was sore from rubbing and your nose was tired of smelling.

Oh, it's true that your spirits were raised when your little granddaughter smiled at you while her brother handed you the jar of jelly beans. And you think of them whenever you notice the jelly beans on your desk. But the high moments of their visit came when the little girl squealed with delight as you read to her and helped her rub those spots in the book.

You may have a rather sublime feeling when you remember your grandson's words when he handed you the jar of jelly beans. But it can't match the elation you feel when you relive the fun you shared over the gifts to them. And, too, your memory includes the fun of buying the beach ball for the boy and selecting just the right book for the little girl. Yes, the giving experience was richer because you gave a lot of yourself with the book and the beach ball.

Giving a part of yourself when you do something for someone may be called the *priceless ingredient* of giving. No one has expressed it better than James Russell Lowell in Part II, stanza 8, of *The Vision of Sir Launfal*:

Not what we give, but what we share—
For the gift without the giver is bare;
Who gives himself with his alms feeds three—
Himself, his hungering neighbor, and me.

Let's look at that jar of jelly beans again, because the more you do, the more you will understand about the happiness of giving—of doing something for others.

Up to this point, the jelly bean story has been used as an illustration, an example. From here on, it is true. A friend, Marilyn, who lives two streets away in our small town, was given a jar of jelly beans. It may have been a door prize or a gift from a house guest. That doesn't matter. What does matter is the amount of happiness that came out of that jar.

Marilyn was not particularly fond of candy, especially jelly beans. She would eat one every few days, just because they were there. At that rate her supply was due to last for a year or more. Then things changed.

One afternoon she was working with her flowers in the front yard when little five-year-old Wendy from next door wandered over. After the usual helloes, Marilyn remembered the jar of jelly beans.

"Do you like jelly beans?" she asked Wendy.

"Uh-huh."

"Well, go ask your mother if you can have some."

A few minutes later, Wendy returned. In the background, her mother called from her kitchen window, "It's all right for her to have a few jelly beans. But don't let her make a nuisance of herself. If she gets in your way, send her home."

That's how it started, about a year ago. Marilyn took Wendy into her kitchen and gave her some jelly beans. How many? You certainly can't give a child one jelly bean.

So she worked it out this way. "How old are you?" she asked Wendy.

Wendy held up five fingers and said, "Five."

Marilyn gave her five jelly beans.

Ah! It's a well-known fact. When it comes to free food and handouts, little girls and boys are like squirrels and birds and cats. They always come back for more. They develop that habit quickly.

And so, every afternoon for the next two or three weeks, Wendy showed up at Marilyn's kitchen door and said, "Hello."

Then one day, when Marilyn answered the door, two little children stood there—Wendy and a little boy. "He's Bobby," Wendy said, "He's four."

Five jelly beans for Wendy, four for Bobby.

As I said, it started a year ago. The last I heard, the congregation numbered six. The drain on the jelly bean jar now totals twenty-eight a day. Its original contents disappeared long ago, and Marilyn has become the local store's best jelly bean customer.

Can you imagine the amount of love that pours out each day when the jelly beans are so carefully counted out, and the little ones smile and say "Thank you"? Is there any way to measure the joy that fills Marilyn's heart when she does the counting?

The punch line to the story comes from her husband. At a recent dinner party with friends, he put his hand to his forehead in mock agony and said, "Do you have any idea what it means to be married to a neighborhood celebrity? Marilyn is known among the tricycle set as 'the jelly bean lady.'"

That is further proof, if you need it, to show that Jesus was right when he said, "It is more blessed to give than to receive" (Acts 20:35).

Listen to a former President of the United States tell it his way. Woodrow Wilson, speaking to a group of students at Princeton in 1901, gave this testimony from his own experience:

"No thoughtful man ever came to the end of his life, and had time and a little space of calm from which to look back upon it, who did not know and acknowledge that it was what he had done unselfishly and for others, and nothing else, that satisfied him in the retrospect, and made him feel that he had played the man."

This shows that happiness grows and blossoms *as a by-product of service to others.*

So start now. Put your new way of thinking to work and get busy—*doing something for someone else.*

"What can I do?" you ask, "I can't stop my work to run around helping other people all day long. I'm not rich. I don't have a lot of time or money to spend on doing things for people. What am I supposed to do?"

No one can tell you what to do or how to do it. But one fact stands out. You don't need a lot of money to put the

Golden Rule to work. You may not have great material riches to call on, but you do have plenty of heavenly treasures in your storehouse. And a funny thing about them—the more you give away, the more you have.

Service to others begins with thoughtfulness. It can take the form of words or deeds or even something as simple as a smile or a pat on the back. Your words can reach out by mail or by telephone or face-to-face.

It can start any time you wish. One good place to start is in your own home. And the only riches you will need are those Christian attributes you have been practicing.

A husband who has begun to turn his selfish way of thinking into thoughts of others might start right there. He might hang up his own clothes if he is not already doing it, or take out the garbage without being asked. He might even strain himself to open the car door for his wife—as he did years ago on their first date. (That can be dangerous. It might make the neighbors talk. And strangers who see him do it will think he either has a new car or a new girl friend.)

A wife might sew that button on her husband's coat. The one that pulled off a week ago—or was it last year? She might offer to drive her elderly neighbor to the supermarket. Or help in any number of volunteer community service organizations.

Even shut-ins can *do unto others*. A note to a friend in a distant city, or a phone call to someone you haven't seen in weeks, can help you practice *kindness*.

What about sending a compliment to some young person? If you don't know any, read your newspaper. When you read about a teenager who has done something outstanding, cut out the clipping and mail it to him or her. A stranger? Who cares?

Ten minutes of your time might bring hours of joy and pleasure to that young person. Who knows? It might be just the touch that he needs to strengthen his determination to succeed.

If you are looking for an idea, what about remembering your friends on their birthdays? I had a friend, who died several years ago, who called me long distance on my birthday every year. I asked him about it one time. "Years ago," he said, "when I was getting started as a salesman, I began calling customers on their birthdays. The idea made a hit. And I got so much pleasure out of it that I have expanded my list to include friends all over the United States. It's a great hobby. I average about two calls a day."

That might be a bit expensive for you, but you could send birthday cards. You might be surprised how much fun you can give by quietly and unobtrusively building your list of dates.

You can buy beautiful cards in a card shop, or if your list gets large enough, you could have your own printed.

My wife makes her own cards. Her list is long now—several hundred. At the beginning of each year, she writes and designs a new card. Then she produces enough of them for the new year.

There you are!

The Six Steps to Happiness.

The first five steps have prepared you for the exciting call from Jesus himself, who gave us the secret of happiness when he said, that we should treat others the way we ourselves would want to be treated.

* * * * *

What can you do for others? No one can answer for you. You must find your own way. But remember this: The only limits to what you can do are the limits to your own imagination and the determination to

Do It!

Six Steps to Happiness

Happiness is what you are,
not what you have;
What you give,
not what you get;
not what someone does for you
but what you do for someone else.

* * * * *

To find complete happiness in life, listen to the wise teachings of Jesus, and follow these steps:

Step Number One: Make up your mind that you are going to live a happier and fuller and more abundant life. "All things are possible to him who believes" (Mark 9:23).

Step Number Two: Give yourself a sense of purpose. Set a definite goal. "As [a person] thinketh in his heart, so is he" (Proverbs 23:7, KJV).

Step Number Three: Give yourself a sense of direction—a road to follow. "I am the way, and the truth, and the life" (John 14:6).

Step Number Four: Change your way of thinking. Replace your harmful thoughts with beneficial thoughts. "Blessed are the pure in heart, for they shall see God!" (Matthew 5:8).

Step Number Five: Call on God for help. "Ask, and it will be given you; seek, and you will find; knock, and it will be opened to you" (Matthew 7:7).

Step Number Six: Get busy! Action is the key to happiness. "As you wish that men would do to you, do so to them" (Luke 6:31).

Just as *unhappy thinking* can become a devastating habit, *happy thinking* can become a glorious, uplifting habit.

To help you develop that habit, you might want to use a daily work sheet similar to the one below. It can serve as a habit developer, a reminder, a stimulator, and a record.

My Golden Rule Chart

* * * * *

Today, I am going to follow the Six Steps to Happiness.
This is what I plan to do for someone else.
I've even listed them by name.

1. _____

2. _____

3. _____

4. _____

5. _____

This is what I actually did.

1. _____

2. _____

3. _____

4. _____

5. _____

I had a happy day because I remembered that Jesus said I should treat others as I would want others to treat me.

and

I did it!